Unlock Grace Power

How to Take the Kingdom of God by Force

A Short Read
by

Chris **Cree**

UNLOCK GRACE POWER: How to Take the Kingdom of God by Force

Published by SuccessCREEations, LLC

CONTENTS

Chapter 1
Our Mindsets Matter

"For as he thinks in his heart, so is he."
— Proverbs 23:7a

Mission Trip Experience

Early on in our marriage I was blessed with the opportunity on two different occasions to go to Brazil on mission trips. The second time Lisa was able to go on the trip too. In the two short weeks she was there, Lisa managed to learn to communicate remarkably well with the Brazilians in Portuguese.

She probably learned about 500 words. Her accent was good too. So much so, that one of the workers where we stayed was sure Lisa had studied Portuguese in university. He couldn't believe Lisa picked up so much of the language so quickly.

I, on the other hand, didn't even learn 50 words despite being immersed in the language twice as long as Lisa was.

Why such a big difference between how much of the language we were able to speak? How was Lisa able to learn more than ten times as many words as I did in half the time?

Was it because Lisa is better with languages than me?

She might be. But when I looked back on that time, I see Lisa and I had very different mindsets about the whole thing.

Lisa just plowed in and tried to speak Portuguese. She knew she'd probably say things wrong at first. And she did. But she had a healthy mindset about the whole thing and chose to laugh at her mistakes and keep trying.

And with some of her mistakes, *everyone* was laughing. There were a couple times what she said was horribly, and hilariously, wrong.

Unfortunately for me, my mindset held me back. You see I didn't want to say anything unless I could say it exactly right. Therefore I didn't try to speak even a tiny fraction of the amount that Lisa did.

My mindset told me I wouldn't be able to do it. As a result I wasn't willing to take the risk of saying something wrong. That fear of making mistakes held me back, and meant I learned very little of the language.

Lisa's mindset said she would give it her best shot, learn from her mistakes, and enjoy the experience along the way. She knew she would likely say things wrong. And she knew that was the only real path to learning how to say things right.

That's just one example of how different mindsets going into a situation can produce radically different results.

Our Mindsets Determine Our Outcomes

The Bible tells us that as a man thinks in his heart, so is he (Proverbs 23:7).

Our mindsets are vitally important.

Here is how the word mindset is defined:

1. A mental attitude or inclination

2. A fixed state of mind

What we think about ourselves in our hearts really determines our identity. What we believe about ourselves really does have a massive impact on what outcomes we experience in any given situation.

Henry Ford famously said, "Whether you think you can or think you can't — you're right."

Our mindsets are far more important to us than many appreciate. This is why the Bible tells us to guard our hearts. For example,

> *Keep your heart with all diligence,*
> *For out of it spring the issues of life.* — Proverbs 4:23 (NKJV)

That word "keep" means to set a watch over. That's not talking about a wristwatch. It's telling us to place a guard over our hearts, and to be vigilant about it too.

The word "issues" refers to borders, boundaries, or extremities.

The idea is that we need to pay close attention to the condition of our hearts because it is our heart's condition that ultimately determines how big our influence is for the Kingdom of God.

Look at how the New Living Translation renders that verse,

> *Guard your heart above all else,*
> *for it determines the course of your life.* — Proverbs 4:23 (NLT)

It's an exhortation to protect our own hearts above everything else because our heart is what sets the course of our lives. Not only does our heart determine where we go, it also sets the limit on how far.

People tend to think it is outside forces that limit how far we can go. The world will tell you that factors such as your skin color, current economic status, the country you were born in, how much formal education you have, or your family situation are what control how far you go in life. But when it comes to reaching our ultimate destiny, the Bible shows us those external factors are all secondary to the internal condition of our hearts.

Jesus said it this way,

> *A good man out of the good treasure of his heart brings forth good; and an evil man out of the evil treasure of his heart brings forth evil. For out of the abundance of the heart his mouth speaks.* — Luke 6:45 (NKJV)

Our heart determines the kind of person we are, not external factors. Jesus uses the word "treasure" to describe what our heart contains. That means it's valuable. It's also abundant, because the word He uses refers to a treasury or a storehouse.

Jesus adds two more important points about our mindsets for us to consider in the last sentence of that passage.

First, by using the word "abundance," Jesus reveals there is so much treasure in our hearts, that we effectively draw from the overflow. There is far more treasure available in our hearts to keep drawing from than the leftover bits we release into our world.

The final bit is the mechanism by which the treasure in our hearts is converted into our destiny. According to Jesus, the words we speak make all the difference. In context, Jesus is talking about the fruit produced in our lives.

Importance of Our Words

The words we say are a mirror into the condition of our hearts. That means we can often discern what we really believe by listening to what we say as we go about our daily routine.

Here's a thought experiment that might be a bit disturbing for some. Imagine a clerk followed you around all day, every day, and recorded every single word you said.

What would they record you saying to your spouse, or your children? What would they hear you say to people at work, or at church? What do you say to yourself?

Are the words you speak uplifting and encouraging to all those people? Are they full of faith and hope? Or do you tend to tear people down with words of fear, doubt, and unbelief? Are you encouraging to others, only to tear yourself down on a regular basis?

Perhaps it might be time for a change in mindset. If you see a problem in this area, you will do well to correct it as quickly as possible. In the parallel passage in Matthew, Jesus gets more specific about our spoken words,

> *But I say to you that for every idle word men may speak, they will give account of it in the day of judgment.* — Matthew 12:36 (NKJV)

That's a sobering prospect to consider. Listening to our own words is a good self-test to measure the status of our hearts. The first step in solving a problem is to realize the problem exists. Only after we see a problem can we move forward with a solution.

Time For Kingdom Mindsets

If you are just now realizing that you've got an issue with your mindset based on the words you say, I've got some good news for you. You can change your mindset!

That's what the discipleship process is all about, changing our mindsets. Look at this passage,

> *And do not be conformed to this world, but be transformed by the renewing of your mind, that you may prove what is that good and acceptable and perfect will of God.* — Romans 12:2 (NKJV)

When we renew our minds, it changes our mindsets. Doing that allows us to know, understand, and demonstrate to others what God's will is.

Basically, we want to start thinking godly thoughts and responding in godly ways. To start thinking God thoughts we must change where we focus our attention.

There's truth in the saying that we become like the people we spend the most time with. The only way we can to change our thinking patterns for the better is to spend more time in God's presence learning His thoughts.

The best way to do that is to spend time studying the Bible, because the Bible is God's Word after all. At the same time we need to take what we read in the Bible back to God Himself and let the Holy Spirit teach us the meaning of what we're reading and how He wants that to transform our own lives.

By doing so we activate a powerful combination in our lives of studying the very words of God coupled with real relationship with Father God. Then we let God and His words change us into His own image.

It takes some effort to slow down and truly seek God. Most of all it takes some time.

But when we are consistent about building time for both of those things in our lives we will change. We will be transformed from the inside out. You probably won't even notice it at first. But eventually you'll run into something that used to totally rock your world and find you handle it with a loving grace you didn't realize was in you.

I like how the Message paraphrases that verse in Romans.

> *Don't become so well-adjusted to your culture that you fit into it without even thinking. Instead, fix your attention on God. You'll be changed from the inside out. Readily recognize what he wants from you, and quickly respond to it. Unlike the culture around you, always dragging you down to its level of immaturity, God brings the best out of you, develops well-formed maturity in you.* — Romans 12:2 (MSG)

Our goal is to replace our worldly mindsets with Kingdom mindsets. Look at this definition of the Kingdom:

1. The eternal Kingship of God
2. The realm in which God's will is fulfilled

That's why I like the term Kingdom Mindsets. It sums up our ultimate goal in discipleship. We are changing our mental attitudes or inclinations to enter into the realm in which God's will is fulfilled.

With that in mind, let's look at some specific mindsets in the next chapter.

Prayer

Father, thank you for creating my heart with so much power that it sets the course of my life. Thank you for giving me a window into my own heart through the words I say to myself and others. Show me how to renew my mind with new Kingdom mindsets and transform my heart so it charts a new course to the destiny you have planned for me.

Chapter 2

Mindsets of Slaves vs. Sons

"Therefore you are no longer a slave but a son, and if a son, then an heir of God through Christ"
— Galatians 4:7

Importance of Identity

Many believers today do not understand that they have been adopted into God's family as His very own son or daughter. And for many who do know this, it's more of a fact in their brains than a reality in their experience.

How can I say something like that?

Well, we can get a good sense of what someone's mindset is by looking at the fruit in their lives. For much of the body of Christ, the fruit being produced is more consistent with mindsets of slaves than mindsets of sons and daughters.

This isn't a book about our identity. Even so, our identity is everything. Everything we do, everything we are, how we relate to other people, how we respond to the pressures of life, and what we ultimately will achieve and become — all of that and more — ultimately flows from our identity.

As we talked about in the last chapter, how we view ourselves, how we think about ourselves and what we believe in our hearts, is what determines our destiny.

Hopefully you can see that someone with the mindsets of a slave will have a very different destiny than someone with mindsets of an heir of God through Christ.

So let's talk about these different mindsets and see which are more in line with who the Bible says we are in Christ.

Slaves Begging for Mercy

Many believers today approach God as if they were slaves begging for mercy. Yet the Bible paints a very different picture of how we are to approach God.

> *Let us therefore come boldly to the throne of grace, that we may obtain mercy and find grace to help in time of need.* — Hebrews 4:16 (NKJV)

That's not describing a timid slave begging. Our mindset should be that of a son or daughter coming to our good Father in Heaven to boldly ask for what we need.

Notice that we still do get mercy. Yet our mindset makes all the difference. Instead of begging for help with barely the faintest hope that we'll receive it, we ask boldly, knowing God already promises to give us the help we need.

Coming boldly before the throne to ask God for help may be perceived as presumptuous to some. If it sounds that way to you, that's a sign you are working through some of these slave mindsets.

If that's the case, please be encouraged in knowing I still struggle with this some myself. Like you, I am a work in progress and am growing in this area. And I suspect most believers have moments when they feel unworthy to ask God for help.

That will happen whenever we take our eyes off Jesus and lose sight of the fact that it is His worthiness and His righteousness that gives us the right to stand before the Father with our requests. Jesus is worthy. And we are in Him. Therefore we are now worthy too.

It is never presumptuous to receive something God already promises to give us.

Slave Mindsets

With that said, let's look at some of the mindsets of a slave.

Slaves are Submissive — Slaves have no autonomy because they are property. They have no freedom to choose what to do. Instead they must do what their masters tell them, or they will suffer the consequences.

Slaves are Fatalistic — Because they have no autonomy, slaves tend to take on an attitude that whatever happens was meant to be. "It is what it is" might be their catch phrase.

Slaves are Passive — Slaves don't take initiative because they don't know their master's business. When slaves finish their assigned tasks they stop and wait for the next thing they are told to do. For the slave, doing nothing is far better than doing the wrong thing. Slaves don't ask "why?" It doesn't matter if what they are told makes no sense to them. They don't get to question it.

Slaves are Fearful — Slaves live in fear of punishment for their mistakes. So much so, that this is their primary motivation for doing good work. They tend to view doing nothing as better than doing the wrong thing because they are more afraid of being punished for doing something wrong than for passivity.

Slaves are Poverty Stricken — Slaves are given just enough provision by their masters to complete their assigned task and survive. Because they are property of their masters, slaves can't really own anything themselves. This causes them to have all sorts of poverty mindsets where the focus is primarily on survival.

Unfortunately, far too many Christians have these same mindsets when it comes to their own identity and their relationship with God.

Slaves to Sin

One problem is every one of us was born into slavery. The Bible tells us that when we were in Adam, before we were born again in Christ, we were slaves to sin. Slavery is all we knew.

Because slavery is their identity, many just shift their slavery status from being a slave to sin over to being a slave to God. And they even look to the Bible to reinforce this slave identity.

In fact, here is the heading written in my New King James Version Bible at Romans 6:15,

From Slaves of Sin to Slaves of God

And reading through the passage is does at first appear that we are indeed slaves to God. However, look at verse 19,

> *I speak in human terms because of the weakness of your flesh. For just as you presented your members as slaves of uncleanness, and of lawlessness leading to more lawlessness, so now present your members as slaves of righteousness for holiness.* — Romans 6:19 (NKJV)

Here Paul clearly says he is using a crude illustration because we are not getting his point. This is not the end of what Paul has to say on the subject by any means.

In fact, if we keep reading through the book of Romans, we will read through the entirety of chapter seven. There, Paul talks about the futility of keeping the Law to produce righteousness because of our absolute inability to keep it.

Yet we must keep reading still further down into chapter eight where we eventually come to this,

> *For as many as are led by the Spirit of God, these are sons of God. For you did not receive the spirit of bondage again to fear, but you*

> *received the Spirit of adoption by whom we cry out, "Abba, Father."* — Romans 8:14-15 (NKJV)

We are no longer slaves to sin. We are set free from that bondage. Unfortunately, many, many Christians put themselves back into bondage again, even after they have been set free.

Paul wrote the book of Galatians to confront this very problem. There he warns us not to go back to that mess and put ourselves under that yoke of bondage anymore,

> *Stand fast therefore in the liberty by which Christ has made us free, and do not be entangled again with a yoke of bondage.* — Galatians 5:1 (NKJV)

But, as we saw back in Romans chapter eight, we're in an even better position than that. Not only are we set free, but then God does the unthinkable. He adopts us former slaves into His very own family.

We are no longer in bondage to the spirit of fear. Now we have received the spirit of adoption.

In Romans chapter eleven Paul uses the imagery of branches being grafted into an olive tree to help explain how we have been grafted into God's family. Israel was God's original family. However, many of the Jews rejected Jesus. Therefore Paul says those unbelieving Jews were broken off the tree.

By faith, we have been grafted into God's family in their place.

You are now a son or a daughter of God and not a slave anymore! This is why Jesus refers to Him as the Father.

Note About Being Sons

I should mention that Paul uses the term "sons" to describe our position instead of "sons and daughters." This is not degrading to women in any way. In fact it's just the opposite. Let me explain.

In the culture of that day, women were second class citizens. As an example, inheritance was passed down through sons, not daughters.

Jesus was radical in that He allowed women to learn at His feet right along with men. That wasn't the norm in that culture.

Yet Paul tells us that we, *"are all sons of God through faith in Jesus Christ"* (Galatians 3:26). Then he goes on to say,

> *There is neither Jew nor Greek, there is neither slave nor free, there is neither male nor female; for you are all one in Christ Jesus.* — Galatians 3:28 (NKJV)

Paul is not making a statement about biology when he says there is neither male nor female. Nor is he denying that humans come in both male and female form. Instead, it's an emphatic statement that there are no class considerations when it comes to believers. In the Kingdom of God there is no longer any distinction between Jews and non-Jews, between slaves and free people, between Americans, Africans, and Asians, nor between men and women. Once we are in Christ, each of us now has the same exact direct access to God through Jesus as any other believer.

We also have the same potential for authority in the Body of Christ too, regardless of whether we are male or female. So those that think women cannot be leaders in the Kingdom of God are completely off base.

By calling us all "sons of God" Paul elevated the status of women from second class citizens to co-equal with men. If He had said "sons and daughters of God" in that culture, at that time, he would have kept the two-tier class system in place.

Therefore, when we see "sons of God" in the New Testament, we can know it translates into "sons and daughters of God" in our culture today.

Mindsets of Sons

Now that we have established our rightful position in God's family because of Jesus, let's look at how the mindsets of sons are different from slave mindsets.

Sons are Bold — Sons are grounded in their father's love. That gives them a confidence and boldness to move forward, knowing their father has their back with their best interest in mind.

Sons are Optimistic — The love of their father gives sons a positive outlook where they come to expect good outcomes, regardless of whatever circumstances they find themselves in.

Sons are Proactive — Sons are in the know when it comes to their father's business. Therefore, they step in and step up when they see something that needs doing rather than waiting passively for someone to give them instructions.

Sons are Courageous — Sons are willing to take risks to see bigger rewards. Again, it goes back to their security in their father's love. This combined with the knowledge that their father has all the resources they need to accomplish whatever task is at hand, gives them courage to accomplish big things for their father's business.

Sons are Prosperous — Sons have access to all the resources available in their father's estate. They are free to be generous on every occasion in the knowledge their father has both the means and willingness to back them, no matter what.

The question "why?" is very important to sons. The reason behind what they are instructed to do is often even more important than the task itself. That's why Jesus said,

> *No longer do I call you servants, for a servant does not know what his master is doing; but I have called you friends, for all things that I heard from My Father I have made known to you.* — John 15:15 (NKJV)

In that passage, Jesus elevates us from servant status because He makes known to us what the Father is doing. And as we've already shown in this chapter, not only are we friends of Jesus, we are also adopted sons of God, making Him our Father too!

All that to say, God wants to include you in on what He is doing in the world. You are His precious child and not His slave. He longs to have an intimate relationship with you where He can both bless you, and at the same time bless others through you.

Set aside any slave mindsets you have and take on the mindsets of a son of the Most High God. Join in the family business of expanding the Kingdom of God throughout the world!

Prayer

Jesus, thank you for accomplishing everything needed for me to be worthy of adoption into God's family as His very own son through Your finished work on the cross and Your resurrection. Father, right now I repent from any passive, fearful slave mindsets I've allowed to creep in along with any thoughts of unworthiness. I know that because Jesus is worthy, that means I too am worthy because I am in Him. Today I choose to take on the Kingdom mindsets of Your child and one of Your heirs through Jesus.

Chapter 3
Crippling Passivity

"For if you remain completely silent at this time, relief and deliverance will arise for the Jews from another place, but you and your father's house will perish. Yet who knows whether you have come to the kingdom for such a time as this?"
— Esther 4:14

The Problem of Passivity

Passivity is crippling much the Body of Christ today. This passivity and the fatalistic mindsets of slaves adopted by many believers causes them to withdraw into their church community and refrain from engaging culture.

Part of the problem has to do with the way gospel is presented today. Far too often what's proclaimed is a gospel of salvation, entirely focused on whether we will go to heaven or hell when we die. As a result, many believers see the Kingdom of God as something that is relevant only for eternity, with little application for this life.

Yet when we read through the gospel accounts in scripture with an eye to see, we realize that the Kingdom of God is the gospel Jesus preached. Salvation is just the doorway into the Kingdom. There is so much more to it, including a great deal which makes our lives so much better and more meaningful here in this age, as well as once we step into eternity.

Another problem that contributes significantly to the passivity of so many believers today is the extreme sovereignty of God theology which claims God controls everything that happens in our lives here on earth.

Passivity is just one of the problems created by this misunderstanding of God's nature and character. In fact, this misguided theology is such a big problem in the Body of Christ today that I wrote my *Sovereignty of God: Is God Really In Control?* book specifically to address this issue by sharing what the scriptures say about it.

My point is this. A great many believers are very passive, which is a mindset of a slave. This passivity and withdrawal from the culture is a huge contributing factor to the mess our world is in right now. Corruption of the worst kind seems to have permeated every aspect of our society.

The only way things will turn around is if godly men and women step into these situations and bring God's presence, wisdom, peace, and solutions into them.

Age Old Problem

It probably shouldn't be a surprise that so many believers take on a passive mindset. After all, Adam did the same thing in the Garden of Eden.

> *Then the woman saw that the tree was good for food and delightful to look at, and that it was desirable for obtaining wisdom. So she took some of its fruit and ate it; she also gave some to her husband,* ***who was with her****, and he ate it.* — Genesis 3:6 (HCSB)

Adam was standing right there next to Eve when she was deceived by the serpent, and he passively said nothing to confront those lies and deception. Passivity has been an ongoing problem with humanity since the very beginning.

Jesus Praises Boldness

Jesus repeatedly praised people for their boldness. He tended to praise the faith of those who boldly came to Him. This, often despite the disciples feeling bothered by those seeking Jesus. To be fair, some were a bit obnoxious in how they went about getting Jesus' attention.

For example, once a Canaanite woman came to Jesus to get healing for her daughter. Jesus initially refused her because His ministry assignment while on earth was to the Jews, not the Gentiles. Because she boldly (and somewhat loudly) persisted, Jesus relented and,

> *Then Jesus answered and said to her, "**O woman, great is your faith!** Let it be to you as you desire." And her daughter was healed from that very hour.* — Matthew 15:28 (NKJV)

Another time a blind beggar — the Bible calls him blind Bartimaeus — heard that Jesus was passing with His disciples along with what the Bible says was "a great multitude." Blind Bartimaeus started shouting after Jesus, hoping to get His attention. People tried to get him to stop making so much noise.

As before, Jesus acknowledged Bartimaeus' faith.

> *Then Jesus said to him, "Go your way; **your faith has made you well.**" And immediately he received his sight and followed Jesus on the road.* — Mark 10:52 (NKJV)

These are just two of a great many examples where Jesus praised people's boldness in the gospel accounts. Often He tied that boldness to their expressions of faith as He performed miracles on their behalf.

Jesus Condemns Passivity

In addition to praising boldness, Jesus also had some very harsh things to say about passivity.

The parable of the talents is one example. In this parable, we see two servants get rewarded for risking the money their master gave them and turning a profit in the marketplace. However, the third servant had a passive mindset and buried his master's money in the ground until the master returned.

That third passive servant is called "wicked and lazy."

> *"But his lord answered and said to him, '**You wicked and lazy servant**, you knew that I reap where I have not sown, and gather where I have not scattered seed. So you ought to have deposited my money with the bankers, and at my coming I would have received back my own with interest.'"* — Matthew 25:26-27 (NKJV)

In the verse immediately before that passage, we see what thinking caused the passivity,

> *And **I was afraid**, and went and hid your talent in the ground. Look, there you have what is yours.* — Matthew 25:25 (NKJV)

He was afraid. Just like with that servant in this parable, fear is often underlying the passive mindset with believers today. Keep in mind, fearfulness is also a slave mindset.

And, just as in the parable, the hidden problem behind the fearful passivity of believers is that we don't really know the true nature and character of either Jesus or the Father.

Fear leads to passivity and cowardice. Cowardice is explicitly condemned in the New Testament. So much so, that the cowardly will be first in line to spend eternity in the lake of fire at the end of the book of Revelation.

> *But the cowardly, unbelieving, abominable, murderers, sexually immoral, sorcerers, idolaters, and all liars shall have their part in the lake which burns with fire and brimstone, which is the second death.* — Revelation 21:8 (NKJV)

Obviously, Jesus sees passivity as a very serious problem.

Antidote to Passivity

Intimacy with God is the solution to this problem because understanding God's character and nature can only flow out of an intimate relationship with Him. It's in that relationship where we gain a true revelation of His love for us. As we do, we begin to experience His goodness and see all the good plans He has for us. Plus, that's where we can begin to walk in the outrageously abundant life God makes available to us through His promises.

Only then do we begin to leave fearful passivity behind and start to experience a powerfully faith-filled, boldly proactive adventure with God.

John says it this way,

> *There is no fear in love; but perfect love casts out fear, because fear involves torment. But he who fears has not been made perfect in love.* — 1 John 4:18 (NKJV)

This is what Paul was getting at when he tells us,

> *Now to Him who is able to do exceedingly abundantly beyond all that we ask or imagine, according to the power that works in us.*— Ephesians 3:20 (MEV)

God's power is in His grace. That power works within us through the release of our faith. It works through us, but only with our cooperation.

When that power of God's grace combines with our faith and begins working in our lives, God is able to accomplish immeasurably more than anything we can ask of Him. In truth, God is ready and able do far more than anything we can even imagine asking of Him.

God has already done His part. The grace is there, available to anyone willing to receive it. When we become fully persuaded God is able to perform what He promises, then we unlock grace power in our lives and things will start to change in our world.

Far from being passive, the Christian faith is designed to be proactive and productive. Let's look at some examples.

True Faith Produces Works

Faith is an action word. This trips some people up because they think faith involves believing harder and waiting for God to do something.

In reality, Jesus already accomplished everything we need to experience the fullness of the Kingdom of God right now. So God's already done His part.

The way we release faith is by taking action, meaning we do something or say something that aligns with scripture. James says it this way,

> *Thus also faith by itself, if it does not have works, is dead. But someone will say, "You have faith, and I have works." Show me your faith without your works, and I will show you my faith by my works.* — James 2:17-18 (NKJV)

Unless our faith moves us to take some sort of action, it's dead, or not really faith at all. Since faith produces works, it cannot be passive.

In fact, Hebrews chapter eleven is a passage which is often called the faith hall of fame. There we see a big list of things done by people of God, going all the way back to Abel from Genesis chapter four. This record of mighty exploits in the book of Hebrews chronicles a great many boldly proactive men and women.

These accounts of faithful exploits are set before us to reveal how true faith produces works.

True Love Produces Works

Love is an action word too. Contrary to what many believe, love is not just an emotion or a warm, fuzzy feeling. Love is a deliberate choice to do something for someone else.

John says it this way,

> *But whoever has this world's goods, and sees his brother in need, and shuts up his heart from him, how does the love of God abide in him? My little children, let us not love in word or in tongue, but in deed and in truth.* — 1 John 3:17-18 (NKJV)

Love isn't just about lip service. Instead, true love produces good deeds. We know this because Jesus is the pinnacle example of what love looks like.

> *But God demonstrates His own love toward us, in that while we were still sinners, Christ died for us.* — Romans 5:8 (NKJV)

Jesus said it this way,

> *For God so loved the world that He gave His only begotten Son, that whoever believes in Him should not perish but have everlasting life.* — John 3:16 (NKJV)

God loved, so He gave. Expressing generosity is a big way we can show love for God and love for others.

Love demands action. If we believe love can be expressed passively, we are deceived. John even says that true love requires more than words. That's something to think about.

Receiving God's Grace Produces Holiness

Some believers have a twisted view of God's grace. They presume that because God loved us when we were still sinners, and because we did nothing to deserve that love, then there is no reason or value for personal holiness in our lives.

Nothing could be further from the truth.

Yes, it is true that our eternal destination is not decided by our behavior, but only by whether or not we put our faith in Jesus and what He did.

Even so, the Bible tells us a huge reason for personal holiness is to make it easier for others to see God.

> *We live in such a way that no one will stumble because of us, and no one will find fault with our ministry.* — 2 Corinthians 6:3 (NLT)

When we live in ungodly, worldly ways, we put up a barrier of hypocrisy that hinders people from receiving Jesus. I know this from personal experience because I turned my back on God for many years because of massive hypocrisy I saw in some Christians around me in high school and college.

Not only that, but far from being an excuse to neglect personal holiness, the Bible reveals God's grace is the very thing that produces holiness in our lives.

> *Therefore do not let sin reign in your mortal body, that you should obey it in its lusts. And do not present your members as instruments of unrighteousness to sin, but present yourselves to God as being alive from the dead, and your members as instruments of righteousness to God. For sin shall not have dominion over you, for you are not under law but under grace.* — Romans 6:12-14 (NKJV)

All the twisted, ungodly behavior which sin produces in our lives no longer has any power over us because God's grace empowers us to live righteously instead. When we genuinely receive God's grace in our lives, it produces holiness.

True Discipleship Produces Obedience

Obedience is yet another area of confusion for some. Some mistakenly believe that, because God loves everyone, and because His grace provides forgiveness for every sin through Jesus, therefore obedience to God doesn't matter. They might claim, "God will just forgive me anyway, so what difference does it make?"

In truth, obedience is vital. Look at what Jesus says,

> *"Not everyone who says to Me, 'Lord, Lord,' shall enter the kingdom of heaven, but he who does the will of My Father in heaven."* — Matthew 7:21 (NKJV)

Jesus isn't about lip service. He expects those of us who follow Him to also do what He says. Obedience is so important to Jesus that He also says it is the one way to show we love Him,

> *If you love Me, keep My commandments.* — John 14:15 (NKJV)

> *If you keep My commandments, you will abide in My love, just as I have kept My Father's commandments and abide in His love.* — John 15:10 (NKJV)

The way we get to that obedience is through discipleship.

> *So you must live as God's obedient children. Don't slip back into your old ways of living to satisfy your own desires. You didn't know any better then.* — 1 Peter 1:14 (NLT)

According to Peter, obedience is something we learn once we follow Jesus. It's part of the discipleship process.

It's also how we fight the good fight of faith as we confront the enemy to enforce the victory Jesus won on our behalf.

> *For the weapons of our warfare are not carnal but mighty in God for pulling down strongholds, casting down arguments and every high thing that exalts itself against the knowledge of God, bringing every thought into captivity to the obedience of Christ.* — 2 Corinthians 10:4-5 (NKJV)

It is vital that we monitor and manage our thoughts. Our thoughts become our words. Our words become our actions. We do well to address the problem at its source, rather than trying to cover up the symptoms.

Entertaining thoughts that are contrary to the truth of the Bible is incredibly toxic and destructive. That's how we end up saying and doing bad things.

However, when we do take every thought captive to the obedience of Christ, then the words we say begin to change. When that happens, it isn't long before our actions begin to change for the better too.

And when that happens, passivity fades as our we become more proactive. That's when things start to improve in our world.

Finally, obedience to God is the path to loving other believers. John says it this way,

By this we know that we love the children of God, when we love God and keep His commandments. For this is the love of God, that we keep His commandments. And His commandments are not burdensome. — 1 John 5:2-3 (NKJV)

The Proactive Way

Hopefully you can see how big a problem passivity is for us believers if we fall into it. Jesus and the first disciples showed us a very proactive way to relate to God.

Jesus certainly was not being passive when He chased all the money changers out of the temple. Did you know He did that twice?

The first time is recorded at the beginning of His ministry in John chapter two. In this instance we know it was something Jesus thought about and deliberately decided to do.

John tells us that after Jesus saw the money changers doing business in the temple, He took the time to braid a whip of cords. He had time to think about what He was going to do while He made a weapon to use.

Nothing about that whole scene is passive.

Then the other three gospels record Jesus throwing the money changers out of the temple a second time in the week before He was crucified.

Jesus is our example. He shows us the proactive way to move forward in the things of God. Perhaps it's time for you to leave your old passivity behind too.

Prayer

Father, I see there are areas in my life where I have let passivity cripple my effectiveness. In some ways I have buried my talents instead of stepping out and risking using them more fruitfully. Holy Spirit, I ask you to fill me with boldness as I choose to face whatever fear comes against me. Father make me aware of Your perfect love which surrounds me and drives out that fear as I begin to take action on the things You show me to do.

Chapter 4
Faith and Belief

"He did not waver at the promise of God through unbelief, but was strengthened in faith, giving glory to God, and being fully convinced that what He had promised He was also able to perform."
— Romans 4:20-21

Testimony

Let's go back in time more than a decade ago. Lisa and I had been believers for more than 15 years at that point in our journey. We were really active in every church we'd been a part of. We volunteered for stuff pretty much every Sunday. And we were generous givers with our finances.

But the reality was, we were frustrated. No matter what we did, we seemed to always be struggling in our lives. In fact, if you were to ask me, I would have been hard pressed to give you any real difference in our lives compared to our unbelieving friends.

I could quote you scriptures about how we were forgiven. And I knew that I'd been set free from alcohol addiction. So there was that. Plus we usually got up a whole lot earlier than our unbelieving friends on Sunday morning so we could go to church.

Beyond that, our lives were little different. We had the same financial struggles as everyone around us. We got sick just as much as anyone else did. We had the same challenges in our relationships with other people.

Where relationships were concerned, I should mention that Lisa and I both have strong personalities. Our strong personalities contributed to what I generally call our "intense fellowships." That just sounds better than saying we argued, even though that's exactly what we did. Way too much.

We were on an emotional roller coaster. Some days things were pretty good, and everything was A-OK. But then other days things weren't so good, if you know what I mean.

I read in the Bible where Jesus said we should come to Him for rest, that His yoke was easy and His burden was light. But honestly, that was pretty much the exact opposite of our own personal experience at that point. To us it seemed like most everything in our Christian walk was really hard. And much of our life was so very heavy.

We would read through the book of Acts. Then we'd look at our own lives. We saw a massive disconnect between our own experience in our lives and what we saw on the pages of scripture.

We felt like we were saved and stuck. We got into the Kingdom of God. We knew we were going to Heaven when we died. But we really weren't experiencing much of the Kingdom in our everyday lives.

Similar Faith and Belief

You see, a big part of my challenge at the time was that I didn't understand the difference between faith and belief. I believed many true things from scripture. But belief doesn't change things, not on its own.

What changes things in our world is faith. I kind of thought that faith and belief were the same thing. But they're not.

What makes it confusing is that faith and belief are very closely related. In fact, the two are so close that they often get confused with each other. Even when we look at the Bible, It can be a little less than clear, depending on the translation you happen to be reading.

For example, let's look at Matthew 17:20. If you remember the story, a man brings his boy to Jesus and says that he first took the boy to the disciples, but they couldn't heal him. After Jesus heals the boy the disciples ask why they couldn't do it. Here's how the New Living Translation presents Jesus' answer,

> *"You don't have enough faith," Jesus told them. "I tell you the truth, if you had faith even as small as a mustard seed, you could say to this mountain, 'Move from here to there,' and it would move. Nothing would be impossible."* — Matthew 17:20 (NLT)

Reading that, it seems like Jesus is telling his disciples that their problem is they don't have enough faith. I mean what else can "you don't have enough faith" mean, right?

But then He goes on to explain the problem of too little faith and how to solve it by saying that we barely need any faith at all to see great miracles happen. What?

That's pretty confusing. Why would He acknowledge that they had any faith at all if His lesson from this particular "teachable moment" was that they only needed a tiny amount of faith?

How much "small as a mustard seed" faith is enough? Presented that way it makes it seem like we need some standard to measure microscopic faith in amounts even smaller than a mustard seed.

I don't know about you, but I can't make any sense of that. Now let's look at how the New King James Version translates that same verse.

> *So Jesus said to them, "Because of your unbelief; for assuredly, I say to you, if you have faith as a mustard seed, you will say to this mountain, 'Move from here to there,' and it will move; and nothing will be impossible for you.* — Matthew 17:20 (NKJV)

Here that same passage appears a whole lot less contradictory. Jesus is telling His disciples that they have a belief problem which can be countered with faith, even in small amounts.

Now that's something we can work with. All we have to do is figure out what belief and faith really are and then we can apply that lesson to our lives.

Translation Differences

But why the difference in the translations?

It turns out there are two main sets of biblical manuscripts that translators work from to bring the English versions of scripture across from the original Greek and Hebrew languages.

These two manuscript sets are almost the same. This verse in Matthew happens to fall into that "almost" area.

The manuscripts used for translations such as the King James Version and New King James Version have the Greek word *apistia* there. That word properly translated means "unbelief" in English.

The manuscripts used for other translations such as the New Living Translation and the New International Version have the Greek word *oligopistia* there instead. That Greek word does not appear anywhere in the other set of manuscripts. It's the noun form of a word that does appear elsewhere in both sets of manuscripts as a verb, and which does mean "of little faith."

Now I don't want to get bogged down in the differences between the manuscript sets and the various translations because my point is this: it is legitimate to understand the problem as one of unbelief instead of one of too little faith. Not only is this a valid translation, but it also enables us to move towards a solution to the problem.

At the end of the day, that's really what I believe we should be focused on — moving forward in the things of God.

Belief Explained

Our beliefs are things that we are thoroughly convinced of. Usually they are ideas and concepts that we gather as we move through life and come across information and experience. In other words,

Our beliefs are opinions or judgments in which we are fully persuaded.

In practical experience our beliefs can, and often do change over time as we gain more knowledge, and as we experience more things throughout our lives.

For example, I was a lot more sure I was right about most things when I was younger. But as I gained more life-experience I have grown to appreciate how much I truly don't know about any given subject.

Here's another way to say it. When I was sixteen I was convinced my father was wrong about a whole host of things. I confess I thought my dad was pretty idiotic about a bunch of stuff. However, as I got older, it seemed my dad got smarter and wiser about a whole host of things.

It's like my dad was a whole lot smarter guy when I was in my forties than he was back when I was a teenager.

In truth, he didn't really get smarter as I got older. My dad was pretty smart the whole time. Instead it was my belief about his wisdom that changed.

There was a time in my walk with Jesus that I believed the supernatural passed away in the first century with the Apostles because that is what I was taught. That belief matched my experience at the time too.

Eventually I learned that Jesus is still in the supernatural business. As my belief in this area changed, so did my life experiences. Today you would have a very difficult time convincing me that supernatural stuff can't happen because I've now experienced too much of it first-hand.

How Faith is Different

Remember in the last chapter we showed that faith is an action word. And it is directly tied to what we believe. So we can say,

Faith is belief in action with confidence.

If you have more of a mathematical bend, you can think of it like this:

Faith = (Belief x Action x Confidence)

Faith includes our beliefs. But it is bigger than that. As we pointed out in the last chapter, if it doesn't move us to do something or say something — to actually take some kind of action — it's not really faith at all.

James said it this way,

> *So you see, faith by itself isn't enough. Unless it produces good deeds, it is dead and useless.* — James 2:17 (NLT)

Until we take action our "faith" is just a bunch of words. James says that unless faith produces action, it is in fact dead, or not faith at all.

The Confidence Factor

The last part of our whole faith equation is confidence.

Confidence is trust based on knowledge or past experience.

Basically confidence is a measure of how firmly we hold to a particular belief.

So you see how those three things come together to determine our faith at any given time. And hopefully you can now see how belief and faith are interrelated. The difference between the two is subtle. But understanding it brings a whole lot more clarity to things that Jesus said, such as Matthew 17:20 above.

When we believe the truth with enough confidence to take action, we exercise faith. And it doesn't take much of that faith to see huge things happen, even miraculous things.

Now hopefully you can see where unbelief, that is believing things that aren't true — believing lies — completely clogs up the working of our faith. Unbelief prevents us from ever seeing the miraculous in our lives.

Too often we spend time and energy trying to increase our faith when Jesus said that's not really our problem. We pray and plead with God, begging Him to give us more faith.

But our problem is really with unbelief, not a lack of faith.

Unbelief Contributes to a Fearful Mindset

Because the opposite of belief is unbelief, you might think the opposite of faith would be *un*faith. But it's not. The opposite of faith is *fear*.

We might believe all the right things, but still be unwilling to step out in faith to take action because of fear. Fear also clogs up the works and will prevent our faith from working.

We see this when Jairus came to Jesus to ask for his daughter to be healed in Luke chapter eight. Jesus was delayed and someone came from Jairus' house to tell him his daughter died. This is what Jesus told him,

> *But when Jesus heard it, He answered him, saying, "Do not be afraid; only believe, and she will be made well."* — Luke 8:50 (NKJV)

Jesus cautioned Jairus not to be afraid because He knew fear would shut down the faith Jairus had that Jesus could heal his daughter.

Hopefully you can see why unbelief and the fearful mindset of a slave we might take on is so very deadly when we need God's supernatural power working in our lives.

This is why it is so vital for us to renew our minds to the truth of God's word. Part of what that does is push out unbelief as we begin to believe what is true. At the same time, we are planting the truth of God's Word and His promises in the soil of our hearts when we renew our minds to those truths.

Over time that truth rises up in our hearts and begins to make our faith effective. Really what it all comes down to is being fully persuaded of what God says. Paul tells us that Abraham did not waiver in unbelief when God told him he and Sarah would have a child in their old age, despite the physical impossibility of what God promised. Then Paul says this about Abraham,

> *He was fully convinced that God is able to do whatever he promises.*
> — Romans 4:21 (NLT)

That is what it looks like when we are in faith. We are fully persuaded that God is willing and able to do whatever He promises. We literally come into agreement with God and what He says in His Word.

That brings us back to my story. What I believed was true, for the most part. But I wasn't taking much (or any) action on what I believed because my confidence was weak. Because I didn't take any action, I wasn't releasing any faith to see Kingdom results.

Fortunately, Lisa and I made the commitment to attend Bible college. We invested the time and effort to renew our minds.

As a result, now we do experience the supernatural in our lives on a regular basis. We have far fewer "intense fellowships" than we did years ago. And the ones we do have are far, far less intense. We've come a long way towards learning how to rest in Jesus and trust Him to produce good outcomes regardless of what things might look like at any given moment.

Best of all, we get to share with others what God has revealed to us. And the people we share with often go on to experience victory too.

The Kingdom of God is amazing!

Prayer

Father, thank you for helping me see the difference between faith and belief. Ignite the passion in me to press even deeper into the truth of Your word so that it pushes out any unbelief that might still be in my heart. As Your truth becomes the foundation of all I believe, give me boldness to step out in faith to help bring heaven to earth as You make me more of a blessing to those around me.

Chapter 5
Receiving God's Grace in Vain

"We then, as workers together with Him also plead with you not to receive the grace of God in vain."
— 2 Corinthians 6:1

A Hard Truth

The Bible reveals a hard truth about my early walk with Jesus. If you remember from the last chapter, at the beginning of my walk with Jesus I didn't experience much of the Kingdom of God in my everyday life.

In reality, I had received the grace of God in vain. Did you know you could do that? That's what Paul says in the Bible I was doing.

> *We then, as workers together with Him also plead with you not to receive the grace of God in vain.* — 2 Corinthians 6:1 (NKJV)

That is a sentence from the Bible which should give you pause.

For starters, that verse completely shuts down the idea that God's grace is automatic. If grace was an irresistible force that automatically affected everyone equally, then it would be impossible to receive it in vain, and this verse would not be in the Bible. But it is. Therefore, God's grace cannot be automatic.

There was something about the church in Corinth that made Paul plead with them not to receive the grace of God in vain. He is urging the church in Corinth to act in accordance with their beliefs.

They were like I was. I had a bit of an understanding of what the Bible said. But I really didn't act on the truth I knew. I had belief, but didn't exercise faith. According to Paul, I was receiving the grace of God in vain.

That's why I was saved and stuck.

Until belief becomes faith it is passive. At that stage what we believe is little more than hope. Hope is good. But until the hope we believe becomes faith, it won't have a very big impact on the world around us.

Waiting on God to Move Us

Unfortunately a large portion of the Body of Christ is doing this very thing. Their passive slave mindsets are causing them to wait for God to do something on their behalf.

They see passages in scripture like Isaiah 40:32 as justification for their passivity.

> *But those who wait on the Lord*
> *Shall renew their strength;*
> *They shall mount up with wings like eagles,*
> *They shall run and not be weary,*
> *They shall walk and not faint.* — Isaiah 40:31 (NKJV)

Many understand that verse to mean that when we sit back and passively wait on God to do stuff, amazing things will happen. I believed that myself for many years, so I appreciate where these folks are coming from.

On the face of it, that verse does appear to sanction passively waiting for God to do something. But let's examine that verse a little more deeply.

The Hebrew word translated "wait" in that verse is קָוָה *qâwâ*. (I'm glad this is a book and I don't have to attempt to pronounce it.)

That Hebrew word literally means to bind together (perhaps by twisting), to collect. The figurative meaning of that word is to wait, look for, hope, or expect. It means to look eagerly for, or lie in wait for.

In truth, there is an active expectancy contained in that word. It's not passive at all.

When we consider what happens as a result, it seems obvious that the waiting should be active too. Think about it.

How would you know if your strength has been renewed if you do nothing that requires strength?

How can you mount up with anything, much less eagle's wings, when you are sitting back?

How would you know if you get weary or faint if you are passively planted, expecting God to move you?

Yes, we wait on God. But we wait expectantly by making ourselves ready to respond the moment God does move on our behalf. I'll share an example what that looks like in a moment.

Empowering Grace

The truth is, God's grace empowers us to step into action. When we act on what we believe, that is faith. And when we step into faith, that is the moment God's grace in our life becomes effective.

Passivity is receiving God's grace in vain.

Paul lays this out more clearly here,

> *But by the grace of God I am what I am, and His grace toward me was not in vain; but I labored more abundantly than they all, yet*

> *not I, but the grace of God which was with me.* — 1 Corinthians 15:10 (NKJV)

Let's unpack that verse a bit.

"By the grace of God I am what I am." Paul was who he was and what he was by the grace of God. You and I are too. The country and family we were born into, our height, eye color, hair color, the way our minds work, the time we were born into, and so much more are all things that we have very little control over.

The fact that I'm naturally an introvert, and Lisa is very much an extravert, are not things that we worked at to achieve. It's just how God wired the two of us.

But God knew exactly what He was doing in each of our lives when He made us, just like He knew what He was doing when He made you. It's God's grace that made us what we are.

Grace Linked to Labor

Then Paul goes on to say, *"And His grace towards me was not in vain; but I labored more abundantly than them all."* Paul ties the grace of God with his own labor. In Paul's case he says he did more work than all the rest.

God's grace empowers you to take action. That grace of God should ignite your faith and launch you into doing something.

One day Lisa and I decided that we were going to do what it took to renew our minds and get off our emotional roller coaster. For us that meant moving across the country to attend Bible college. We believed that spending some concentrated time studying the truth of God's Word would change us.

Boy did it!

Remember this. It's OK if that something your faith launches you to do is a small thing at first. For Lisa and I, the first faith action step we took was to submit our applications to Bible college. Then we put our house up for sale. Then we downsized our lives to move from a house into a smaller apartment. Then we moved across the country to attend school.

We worked and went to school. And we took some money out of our savings to cover some of our costs along the way.

All of these were steps of faith. Each one was an action we took in response to God's grace. And that faith-effort we put in made God's grace effective in our lives.

In the process of all that, God called us to move to Scotland. It would take three and a half years from the time Lisa and I said yes to God's initial call to Scotland before we were able to move there.

Even then there were still steps for us to take so that we would continue towards this assignment God had for us. For example, we needed to raise financial support to get there. To accomplish that, we did all the legal stuff to form a nonprofit and get it registered with the government here in the States.

We put together a comprehensive plan on how we expected to get the Bible college location up and running in Scotland. Then we submitted the plan for approval by that Bible College's organizational headquarters. We then made multiple short-term trips over to Scotland to scout the land. Then there were all the meetings — we had to sort out visas, more planning, downsizing our lives almost completely into a handful of suitcases, and on and on.

And yes, there also was a great deal of waiting for God to sort things out which were completely outside of our control.

Yet the entire time we were waiting, Lisa and I were very actively working on all sorts of preparations so that we would be ready to pull the trigger and move to Scotland at the very moment God sorted those things out which were beyond our control.

God's Grace Working

That brings me to the last thing Paul said in that verse, *"Yet not I, but the grace of God that was with me."*

God's grace is what is at work within us. He's the one who gave Lisa and I the abilities, skills, and talents to do all the things we've done. He gives us favor with people along the way to make our task easier. He even is the one who calls us and anoints us for a particular assignment.

He does the same for every believer.

Don't misunderstand what I am saying here. God absolutely gets all the credit for what we've done.

At the same time, until God's grace is mixed with our faith and we take action, we've still only received God's grace in vain. We must believe the truth that God empowers us to do the things we are called to do so that we can step up and start to do them.

How do we know that's true?

> *I can do all things through Christ who strengthens me.* — Philippians 4:13 (NKJV)

We do the "all things." But we can only do them through Christ who empowers and strengthens us.

Here is another verse that shows God and us working together,

> *Now to Him who is able to do exceedingly abundantly above all that we ask or think, according to the power that works in us.* — Ephesians 3:20 (NKJV)

God is well able to do immeasurably more than all we can ask or even imagine. But He only does so, "according to the power that works in us."

God works through us, with our agreement and cooperation. It is not "all God and none of us." Nor are we going off to accomplish anything of lasting value apart from Him.

Lisa and I based our belief in the truth of God's Word. Then we got into faith and took action. We activated the grace that God already gave us and as a result, like Paul we have not received God's grace in vain.

The truth is this. God's grace has already reached down to you. It's time for your faith to rise up and take action.

Don't hold back waiting for God to show up to do something miraculous. God is already on the inside of you. Wherever you go, He is there by definition. Lean on His strength and power and step into the faith that God's grace supplies.

When you engage your faith and move into action, you will no longer be receiving God's grace in vain.

Prayer

Father, I confess that I have been waiting passively for you to do things on my behalf and move me. I repent of that misguided thinking right now. No longer will I receive Your grace in vain. Instead, I commit to stepping out to take action to move towards the things you've put in my heart. Even though my first steps in that direction may be small, I trust Your grace to work within me as I continue to move forward. I'm excited that You are empowering me to accomplish all that You've put in my heart to do. With each success You bring me, my confidence in You will grow and propel me to take ever bigger steps towards the upward call You place on my life in Christ Jesus.

Chapter 6

The Kingdom Suffers Violence

"And from the days of John the Baptist until now the kingdom of heaven suffers violence, and the violent take it by force."
— Matthew 11:12

John the Baptist's Question

Two of the gospel writers record something interesting which happened between John the Baptist and Jesus.

Keep in mind, these two men were first cousins. John was a few months older than Jesus. They'd known each other their entire lives. John's entire ministry was preparing the way for Jesus.

John was eventually arrested for speaking out against king Herod, because the king had married his own brother's wife. Then Matthew tells us this,

> *And when John had heard in prison about the works of Christ, he sent two of his disciples and said to Him, "Are You the Coming One, or do we look for another?"* — Matthew 11:2-3 (NKJV)

I find it interesting that Jesus didn't directly answer the question. According to Luke it doesn't look like Jesus even attempted to answer the question at first. Instead, He just went about doing His ministry work while John's disciples waited.

Then Jesus answered their question by telling John's disciples to go back and tell him what they saw Jesus do. In that way, Jesus pointed John back to scripture and let scripture answer his question.

Since everything Jesus did were things the Old Testament said the Messiah would do, Jesus confirmed it for John far better with His actions than He would have by just giving a verbal answer.

Profound Statement

This question by John and the visit by his disciples gave Jesus an opportunity to say something remarkably profound.

> *And from the days of John the Baptist until now the kingdom of heaven suffers violence, and the violent take it by force.* — Matthew 11:12 (NKJV)

This verse perplexed me for a long time. At first glance it doesn't make any sense because it sounds like the Kingdom of Heaven will be overrun by violent hostile forces.

But that's not what Jesus was communicating at all. This verse comes in the middle of Jesus talking to the crowd about His cousin John, after John's disciples left.

He was saying the Kingdom of God will not just drop into your lap. Jesus means it takes passion and the willingness to press into God's Kingdom to see its benefits in your life. This falls right in line with something else Jesus said,

> *But seek first the kingdom of God and His righteousness, and all these things shall be added to you.* — Matthew 6:33 (NKJV)

Jesus said that once John the Baptist came on the scene preaching with the power of the Holy Spirit, people were willing to overcome big obstacles and trek way out into the desert to hear John, and receive his message. Since that time passionate people have pressed in to receive and experience the Kingdom of God. Jesus compared their determination to a battle where violent people take the things of God and enter into His Kingdom by force.

A Different Mindset

This idea of taking the Kingdom of God by force is a radically different mindset than many believers have today. But we see that passionate determination to receive a miracle from Jesus repeated throughout the gospel accounts.

I shared in chapter three about the Canaanite woman who wanted healing for her daughter, and about blind Bartimaeus, who wanted his sight. They were both determined to get their miracles from Jesus, regardless of what the people around them thought about their behavior.

Bartimaeus and the Canaanite woman both took the Kingdom of Heaven by force.

One time Jesus was teaching in a crowded house and this happened,

> *Then behold, men brought on a bed a man who was paralyzed, whom they sought to bring in and lay before Him. And when they could not find how they might bring him in, because of the crowd, they went up on the housetop and let him down with his bed through the tiling into the midst before Jesus.* — Luke 5:18-19 (NKJV)

Here are probably four or so guys who have a paralyzed friend. They are so determined to get their friend to Jesus for healing that they climb up on the roof of the house, cut a hole through the roof, and lower their friend down to Jesus.

The next verse tells us that Jesus responded to the friends' faith, not to the faith of the paralyzed man.

We could all use some friends like that who are willing to do whatever it takes to get us in front of the One who can help us.

These friends of a paralyzed man took the Kingdom of God by force.

Another time Jesus was walking through Jericho with His disciples. A guy there named Zacchaeus wanted to see Jesus. Unfortunately for him, he was pretty short and there was a really big crowd drawn to Jesus.

The Bible says Zacchaeus was determined to see Jesus anyway, despite those obstacles. He climbed up a tree to get above the people. Jesus noticed, called him out of the crowd, and went to stay at his house.

> *And he sought to see who Jesus was, but could not because of the crowd, for he was of short stature. So he ran ahead and climbed up into a sycamore tree to see Him, for He was going to pass that way. And when Jesus came to the place, He looked up and saw him, and said to him, "Zacchaeus, make haste and come down, for today I must stay at your house."* — Luke 19:3-5 (NKJV)

As a result, Zacchaeus repented and Jesus said, "Today salvation has come to this house."

Zacchaeus took the Kingdom of God by force.

A man had a son who suffered from seizures which caused the boy to fall into fires and pools of water where he would be burned or could potentially drown.

> *When they reached the crowd, a man approached and knelt down before Him. "Lord," he said, "have mercy on my son, because he has seizures and suffers severely. He often falls into the fire and often into the water. I brought him to Your disciples, but they couldn't heal him."* — Matthew 17:14-16 (HCSB)

When the disciples couldn't heal his son, the man didn't take no for an answer and passively give up. Instead, he made the extra effort to get in front of Jesus. Then Jesus healed his son.

This man took the Kingdom of God by force.

There was a woman who suffered with a bleeding issue for twelve years. The Bible says she spent all the money she had trying to get well. Not only did she *not* get well, but she actually got worse.

Her sickness made her unclean. According to the Law, that meant she had no business being in a big crowd of people. Yet despite this obstacle, the Bible tells us,

> *When she heard about Jesus, she came behind Him in the crowd and touched His garment. For she said, "If only I may touch His clothes, I shall be made well."* — Mark 5:27-28 (NKJV)

This woman snuck up behind Jesus in that massive crowd and received her healing from Him just by touching His clothes. Jesus wasn't even aware of it until it happened.

She took the Kingdom of God by force.

Personal Example

Hopefully you can begin to see that only those who are passionately, and even violently, resolved to receive the best of what God makes available to all of us will experience it.

What does that look like today?

I already gave you some examples. Lisa and I determined to move across the country and attend Bible college. Then we had to overcome a great many more obstacles to fulfill God's assignment to move to Scotland and establish the Bible college campus there.

Just because God gives you a vision or a personal call does not mean it will be easy to fulfill. It will be risky and full of challenges along the way. But it will be possible.

Let me share one more example. A couple months ago, as I'm writing this, I had a bit of a health crisis. Without going into the medical details, let's just say that the symptoms I had were consistent with a variety of issues that ranged in possibility from no big deal all the way up to colon cancer.

It so happens that my grandmother died of colon cancer in her 40's. Isn't it amazing how often our natural mind wants to jump to the worst possible outcome and will try to focus on whatever facts most line up with that worst case scenario?

Fortunately, I know how faith works. So I tried to press into the belief I had and get myself into a place of faith while exercising my authority in Christ to get the symptoms to stop.

By about day three I had to face the reality that my faith wasn't there. So I fessed up to Lisa what I was fighting. In reality, fear was creeping in.

Lisa wasn't going to mess around and said I should see a doctor, which I did. There is no shame in seeking medical help in the natural when our faith is not yet developed enough to receive supernatural healing directly from God.

At the same time, as far as I was concerned personally, everything stopped. I don't mean I stopped living life. In fact, most people around me didn't know anything was going on.

What I mean is that I decided to get serious about moving into a place of faith for healing.

Generally speaking, I've had more revelation in the area of receiving provision from God than I've had when it comes to healing. It wasn't an issue for us in Scotland because God brought us team members who had a big revelation for healing. So I kind of leaned on them in that area.

I needed that to change because I needed personal revelation of my own healing quickly. I committed to pressing into the Kingdom of God and getting a revelation on healing. That became my highest priority.

Lisa agreed with me that everything else I had on my plate could be secondary to pursuing more revelation.

Even though fear came at me hard, I didn't allow myself to panic. I went to some sources I trusted to get some teaching to renew my mind in this specific area.

The Kingdom of Heaven suffers violence and the violent take it by force.

I determined that nothing was going to keep me from seeing full healing, whatever it takes, however long it takes.

A resource that I highly recommend is a book by Teresa Houghteling called *The "Unhealed" Believer*. Teresa's testimony is powerful. And reading her book was a big part of what turned the tide for me. I highly recommend it.

It also helped that Lisa had supernatural faith through those few weeks. That was a tremendous blessing because, truth be told, I really did have some shaky moments in there.

One thing we've experienced in our marriage is that when one of us is struggling, God makes the other one stronger than normal to provide support. This passage in Ecclesiastes has proven very true in our marriage,

> *Two are better than one,*
> *Because they have a good reward for their labor.*
> *For if they fall, one will lift up his companion.*
> *But woe to him who is alone when he falls,*
> *For he has no one to help him up.*
> *Again, if two lie down together, they will keep warm;*
> *But how can one be warm alone?*
> *Though one may be overpowered by another, two can withstand him.*
> *And a threefold cord is not quickly broken.* — Ecclesiastes 4:9-12 (NKJV)

But the point I really want you to get today is this: When you get to that place where you finally decide that nothing will stand between you and whatever promise of God you want to receive, whatever it takes, that is the moment when faith will begin to rise up in your life and things will start to change for you.

In my case, I pressed into the Kingdom of God as hard as I knew how. Despite having a few fearful moments, I wasn't panicked or desperate. I was determined. I was going to receive the healing that was rightfully mine because of what Jesus accomplished on the cross and through His resurrection.

For me, it was less than a month from the time the symptoms started until I got the "all clear" test results from the doctors and the symptoms stopped.

You should know that those symptoms have tried to come back on me. By the time they did I had the confidence to say, "No!" and really mean it. As a result, they left immediately and haven't come back.

It's fairly common for the enemy to try and steal from us, especially after we receive a big victory and experience God's supernatural power working in our lives. Jesus reveals this in His explanation of the parable of the sower where He says,

> *The sower sows the word. And these are the ones by the wayside where the word is sown. When they hear, Satan comes immediately and takes away the word that was sown in their hearts.* — Mark 4:14-15 (NKJV)

Don't be surprised if the enemy comes back at you right after experiencing a supernatural victory. He will try and convince your heart that the victory was a fluke and wasn't real.

As an example, if you received supernatural healing, the enemy might bring the symptoms back a day or so later to try and convince your heart that you aren't really healed.

Fortunately, I was aware of the enemy's schemes in this area. That's why I could stand fast in the knowledge that what God did on my behalf was real, and permanent. God's Word is indeed true, and His promises are powerful.

Now I am confident I will be able to stand firm regardless if those symptoms try to come back again, no matter how many times they might try to come back.

It was some effort to renew my mind to where belief of the truth in this area was established deep down in my heart. But I took the Kingdom of God by force.

Please know this. You cannot be wishy washy and pray, "God, if it's your will…" kinds of prayers and expect to see Kingdom results in your life.

When you get into situations like these, you desperately need to know the promises God makes to you. Because if God already promised it to you in His Word, guess what? It's His will for you to have it!

Maybe the reason you haven't unlocked grace power in your life and don't yet have what you are believing God for is because you haven't been willing to take it by force! How determined are you to experience God's best? What obstacles and excuses are you willing to push aside so that you can lay hold of everything God has made available to you?

Think about that for a moment.

Prayer

Jesus, right now I declare before You and before all of heaven that I am determined take the Kingdom of God by force, just like You showed us to do. I commit to renew my mind to the truth of your word and take possession of the promises the Bible says already belong to me because I am in You. Like blind Bartimaeus, the Canaanite woman, the friends of the paralyzed man, Zacchaeus, and the woman with the issue of blood, I will do what it takes to receive the very best You have for me. I will not let the obstacles that have held me back in the past prevent me from receiving from You, whatever it takes. And I refuse to submit to the lies of the enemy which whisper Your promises aren't really for me. Your word says they are! Therefore, I will receive them!

Chapter 7
Many Called. Few Chosen

"For many are called, but few are chosen."
— Matthew 22:14

Destiny Not Automatic

Some people believe that, for each of us, our destiny will happen completely independent of our input or decisions. They see it as a predetermined outcome totally beyond our power or control.

This is how those who believe God is in control of everything which happens here on earth tend to see destiny. They see passages where Paul uses the word, "predestined," and take those to mean that God arbitrarily predetermines each of our destinies.

Here is one of those passages as an example,

> *For whom He foreknew, He also predestined to be conformed to the image of His Son, that He might be the firstborn among many brethren. Moreover whom He predestined, these He also called; whom He called, these He also justified; and whom He justified, these He also glorified.* — Romans 8:29-30 (NKJV)

God is all-knowing. Because He resides in eternity outside of time, God sees the end from the beginning. That means God knows how we will respond to Him. In this way, God "foreknew" those who will receive Him.

But knowing something will happen is *not* the same thing as causing it to happen.

This passage clearly says God knew in advance that some would choose Jesus; and once they did, He then predestined them to be conformed to the likeness of Jesus. The passage does not say God arbitrarily destines some people to heaven and others to hell. It's not saying that our choices are predetermined. Instead, the passage is saying that the outcomes of our choices are determined in advance.

In truth, we each have some responsibility when it comes to reaching our destiny. We are free to choose. But the consequences of our choices have already been set.

Our responsibility is to choose agreement with God.

Perplexing Verse

There is another verse that perplexed me for a long time. It comes at the end of a parable Jesus tells about a wedding feast, found at the beginning of Matthew chapter twenty-two.

In the parable, a king invited a bunch of guests to attend his son's wedding. But all declined to attend. So he sent his servants back to explain to everyone what a big celebration it was going to be, in hopes that would encourage them to attend.

You can almost imagine them trying to convince the people to attend, "We're talking an extravaganza. The king has spared no expense. There will be a ton of food. It'll be awesome!"

Unfortunately, those invited guests were too busy with their own affairs and still refused to attend. Some even killed the messengers sent by the king. The king was furious and dealt justice to the murders. He says those he invited were not worthy to attend.

Therefore, he sent his servants out to find anyone they could who was willing to attend. Their social status didn't matter. Anyone who would agree to attend the wedding got invited. All those random people the servants encountered, both bad and good, showed up and filled the wedding hall.

Jesus wraps up the story with an encounter between the king and a man "without a wedding garment" who gets thrown out of the celebration.

Jesus sums up the meaning of the parable by saying this,

> *"For many are called, but few are chosen."* — Matthew 22:14 (NKJV)

This statement prompts some questions.

Called and Chosen

What is the difference between being called and chosen? Why are many called, but only few chosen?

Similar to the way the king in the parable opened invitations to the wedding to any who were willing to attend, the gospel invitation is also sent to everyone. We know this because it is not the Father's will that a single person be excluded from His kingdom and perish in the outer darkness of hell. Peter says it this way,

> *The Lord is not slack concerning His promise, as some count slackness, but is longsuffering toward us, not willing that any should perish but that all should come to repentance.* — 2 Peter 3:9 (NKJV)

Paul also tells us it is God's desire for everyone to be saved.

> *For this is good and acceptable in the sight of God our Savior, who desires all men to be saved and to come to the knowledge of the truth.* — 1 Timothy 2:3-4 (NKJV)

Many are called. God's grace has been extended literally to everyone. In fact, John tells us that Jesus paid the price for the sins of the whole world.

> *And He Himself is the propitiation for our sins, and not for ours only but also for the whole world.* — 1 John 2:2 (NKJV)

Propitiation is a theological word that means Jesus is the atoning sacrifice for our sins. He paid everything that was required for everyone in the whole world to experience God's salvation.

However, not everyone wants God. These people who reject God's invitation to salvation because they reject Jesus are represented in the parable above by those guests who outright refused to attend the wedding celebration.

Then there are many others who claim to want God, but do not want to come to Him on His terms. They attempt to get to God through some other path than Jesus. Therefore they are not clothed in His righteousness.

These people receive God's grace in vain, like we discussed in chapter five. They are represented in the parable by the man who was thrown out of the wedding for not wearing proper wedding garments.

Then there are those who are saved, who enter God's kingdom because of their willing acceptance of His sovereign, gracious provision. They freely choose to believe in Jesus and accept the gift of salvation He offers. Paul sums it up for us this way,

> *For the wages of sin is death, but the gift of God is eternal life in Christ Jesus our Lord.* — Romans 6:23 (NKJV)

These people who receive this gift of salvation through Jesus are chosen. Their faith meets God's grace, and that grace is not received in vain. Instead, God's grace is effective, working in them through their faith. In the parable, these are the guests who enjoy the wedding celebration.

Those who are lost are excluded from the Kingdom of God because of their willing rejection of that same sovereign grace. Therefore, of the many who are called, only a few are chosen.

We become chosen when we respond positively to God's call.

Choosing to Be Chosen

Jesus actually uses that same phrase, "many are called but few are chosen," another time. He says it in the lesson from the parable of the workers in the vineyard.

If you remember the story, the owner goes out at the beginning of the day and hires some laborers to work his fields, and they negotiate a specific wage. The landowner then goes out four more times to hire more workers at different parts of the day.

Each of these additional times the owner says he will pay the newly hired workers, "whatever is right," without naming a specific amount.

At the end of the day, the owner pays a full day's wage to everyone hired, including those who only worked an hour. The workers who were hired in the morning and worked the entire day grumbled. But the owner reminded them they agreed on their wage, which he paid them.

Jesus ends this parable by saying,

> *So the last will be first, and the first last. For many are called, but few chosen.* — Matthew 20:16 (NKJV)

Again, the workers who responded to the call and agreed to work the landowner's fields are the ones who were chosen.

How we respond to God determines whether or not we are chosen by Him. We literally get to decide whether we will be chosen.

Keep in mind that God is the one who initiates this process, not us. He calls us first. It is our response to His call that determines whether we are chosen. We only become chosen when we respond positively to Him.

This is yet another example of how the Kingdom of God expects us to proactively respond to God rather than passively sit back and wait for God to do everything. When God's invitation comes, we do well to take it by force.

Become God's Plan A

Not only that, but God continues calling us well beyond our salvation experience.

As a personal example, Lisa and I were chosen for ministry in Scotland simply because we said yes. I know that God called others before us. But they weren't chosen because they didn't respond in faith to that particular call to go to Scotland.

In fact, Lisa asked God about that very thing. Thinking there were others who were called before us, Lisa asked God, "surely we're not your plan A here?"

His response was, *"When you said yes, you became my plan A."*

That's a powerful truth for you to consider because it's the same for you. When you say yes to God, you become His plan A for whatever it is He has for you to do. This is true even if you end up replacing someone else.

We see an example of this very thing in the Bible. Saul was the first one anointed King over Israel. But Saul worried about what everyone else thought of him and let those concerns distract him from faithfully doing things God assigned him to accomplish.

Because of his disobedience, the prophet Samuel says something very significant to Saul.

> *And Samuel said to Saul, "You have done foolishly. You have not kept the commandment of the Lord your God, which He commanded you. For now the Lord would have established your kingdom over Israel forever. But now your kingdom shall not continue. The Lord has sought for Himself a man after His own heart, and the Lord has commanded him to be commander over His*

> *people, because you have not kept what the Lord commanded you."* — 1 Samuel 13:13-14 (NKJV)

We know David was that man after God's own heart referenced in that scripture. David became king over Israel after Saul.

From that passage, it certainly sounds like David is God's plan B and not His plan A.

Yet the book of Revelation tells us that Jesus was, *"slain from the foundation of the world"* (Revelation 13:8). In addition, Peter says this about Jesus,

> *God chose him as your ransom long before the world began, but now in these last days he has been revealed for your sake.* — 1 Peter 1:20 (NLT)

Since Jesus was God's plan of salvation before the world began, and since Jesus was from the line of David, not the line of Saul, that means David really was God's plan A.

Keep in mind that God did not sabotage Saul. Nor did God set him up for failure. Instead, because God is outside of time and sees the end from the beginning, He knew what Saul would eventually do, as well as what he would not do.

God simply made His plans from before time began with that information about Saul in mind. If Saul had chosen the path of obedience instead of expedience, God would have planned on Jesus coming through Saul's lineage instead of David's.

That right there should give you hope. You too can step up and be chosen for whatever assignment God invites you into like David was, and like Lisa and I were. All it takes to be God's chosen plan A is a commitment to continue doing the things God asks you to do. Decide you will respond to God like Isaiah did,

> *Also I heard the voice of the Lord, saying:*
> *"Whom shall I send,*
> *And who will go for Us?"*
> *Then I said, "Here am I! Send me."* — Isaiah 6:8 (NKJV)

Have you received the grace of God? Are you willing to meet God on His terms and submit your life to His truth? If so, you are chosen!

The Kingdom of God suffers violence and the violent take it by force!

God is inviting you to join Him. God isn't trying to do it to you, He wants to do it through you.

In His own sovereign wisdom, God chooses to partner with human beings to accomplish His Kingdom purposes on the earth. You know the invitation God has extended to you to join Him.

It will look different and uniquely personal to you. Odds are He's not asking you to sell everything and move overseas to help disciple a nation. But He might be.

The thing is, you probably already know what invitation, what particular grace, God has extended to you. Respond to that invitation in faith. Take action. Don't receive God's grace in vain.

Prayer

Father, today I say, "yes," to Your call on my life. In doing so, I choose to be chosen. I am humbled by your call, but like Isaiah I say, "Here am I! Send me." I come on Your terms and submit to Your truth. Thank you for making me Your Plan A as I respond in faith to Your divine grace. I believe You will empower me with wisdom, understanding, and ability to accomplish what You are inviting me to do. Your grace towards me will not be in vain because I choose to respond in faith and take action in the direction You are calling me.

Chapter 8
Your Time is Now (Step Up!)

"Now that you know these things, you will be blessed if you do them."
— John 13:17 (NIV)

Led Astray by Google Maps

Lisa and I had been living in Scotland for nearly a year when we were invited to join a visiting minister and his wife for breakfast. These friends of ours were staying in a picturesque place out in the countryside, a ways out from the small town of about 35,000 people where we lived.

We were still very much learning the area, driving on the other side of the road and everything. At that point I still relied heavily on Google Maps to help me get where I wanted to go. I plugged the address into my phone. We picked up a third couple who were joining us for breakfast, and off we went.

About a mile and a half from our destination, the blue line on the map told us to turn down a narrow country lane. Keep in mind, most all the roads in Scotland seem very narrow compared to what Lisa and I were used to in America. But this was more like a driveway than a road. The

Scottish often use the word "wee" to describe something small. In their vernacular, we were on a wee lane.

Since it looked like a driveway, I assumed we were on the driveway into the place where our friends were staying.

At the halfway point, the main lane veered off on a hard right turn. But the blue line said we just needed to go straight for three quarters of a mile and we'd be at our destination. Where it was telling us to go made the wee lane we were on look like Broadway, in comparison.

In fact, it was so narrow and rough looking that I stopped the car, got out, and walked towards it to see if I really wanted to go further. When I did, I saw some fairly fresh tire tracks. So I assumed we were still on the driveway into the place. How bad could it be?

Oh, it was far worse than I could have imagined!

As we got into it in our little Citroën, I realized I'd made a horrible mistake. There were big rocks, tree roots, and bumps, and mud puddles big enough to swallow our entire car. I knew that if I stopped we were going to need a tractor to pull us out. We figured out later that we literally were on a tractor path between two fields which was lined with very old trees on both sides.

But I was already committed. So I pushed down a little harder on the accelerator and did my very best impression of a rally car driver. And we made it through. That was the good news.

The bad news was that I also managed to trash the car in the process. I tore the exhaust system off the bottom of the car, punctured the oil pan, causing all the oil to drain out when I parked the car, and did a bunch of other damage.

The total estimate to repair the car was four times what it was worth. And it was all my fault.

The Power of Blessing

I share that story to encourage you. That was a time when I made a stupid decision that caused a significant problem. I totaled our car.

Fortunately for us, Lisa and I understood that it was really more of God's problem than it was our problem. In fact, those were the first words out of Lisa's mouth when we parked the car. "God, you've got a problem!"

You see we were in Scotland on direct assignment for God. He called us over there. Therefore, He was responsible for our transportation. In our case, that meant we really needed to have a car to fulfill our mission there.

Most people understand how curses work. They believe that someone who is cursed can do everything right and still end up with a bad result because of the curse they are under.

But what many believers seem to miss, is that blessings work the same exact way in reverse. When someone is blessed, they can do everything wrong and still end up with a good result because of the blessing they are under.

The Bible tells us that Jesus redeemed us from the curse and we are now blessed instead (Galatians 3:13-14). And we're not just a little blessed. Look at this,

> *Blessed be the God and Father of our Lord Jesus Christ, who has blessed us with every spiritual blessing in the heavenly places in Christ.* — Ephesians 1:3 (NKJV)

Every possible spiritual blessing now belongs to us because we are in Christ. There is no curse which can overpower God's blessing in our lives. Balaam found that out the hard way,

> *Behold, I have received a command to bless;*
> *He has blessed, and I cannot reverse it.* — Numbers 23:20 (NKJV)

That's exactly what Lisa and I experienced when I trashed that car. In the end, God replaced it with the nicest car we'd ever owned up to that point. He paid for it in cash by directing us to some money I had set aside twenty-eight years earlier, and then promptly forgot about. That was well before I became a believer and years before I met Lisa.

My point is this. God's blessing is more powerful than any curse that might come our way. His blessing is even more powerful than our own mistakes and bad choices.

When we truly believe this, we can boldly step out in faith to do what God is calling us to do because we know that God will bless us even if what we attempt to do falls apart like a Citroën driven down a tree-lined Scottish tractor path. A revelation of the power of God's blessing on your life removes fear of failure, because even if you do it all wrong, you know God will still turn it into a good result somehow.

When we step out in that kind of boldness we begin to take the Kingdom of God by force.

The Power of Repentance

Perhaps you've been tempted to condemn yourself as you've read this book. Maybe you realize that you've been a bit passive in your walk with the Lord. Or you might have discovered some slave mindsets which have been a part of your thinking over the years.

If that is where you find yourself, please resist the condemnation temptation. Instead, I encourage you to simply repent. The moment you change your mind about whatever you realize was wrong in your thinking is the moment everything will start to change in your life.

Repentance is powerful because when you change the way you think, you alter the course of your life. You begin heading in a new direction and will therefore end up in a new destiny.

The simple act of repentance can change sickness into healing. We see this in the life of king Hezekiah. In Isaiah chapter thirty-eight, Hezekiah is very sick, and God instructs the prophet to go and tell the king to get his affairs in order because he is about to die.

Hezekiah responds by praying to God and before Isaiah even gets out of the courtyard of the palace, God tells him to go back to the king and tell him he will instead recover and live another 15 years. The account in Chronicles tells us Hezekiah repented in that prayer (2 Chronicles 32:26).

Repentance can save a city from destruction. We see this in the story of Jonah, who was told to give a warning to Nineveh. The entire city repented, and the city was spared,

> *Then God saw their works, that they turned from their evil way; and God relented from the disaster that He had said He would bring upon them, and He did not do it.* — Jonah 3:10 (NKJV)

Repentance also transformed a murderer into the author of about half the New Testament. Saul of Tarsus was one of those who approved of the stoning of Stephen at the end of Acts chapter seven. Then we see this said about him,

> *As for Saul, he made havoc of the church, entering every house, and dragging off men and women, committing them to prison.* — Acts 8:3 (NKJV)

Saul made it his mission to persecute the church of God and attempted to eliminate all those who followed Jesus. He acknowledged this about himself,

> *For I am the least of the apostles, who am not worthy to be called an apostle, because I persecuted the church of God.* — 1 Corinthians 15:9 (NKJV)

Of course, we know Saul had a life-changing encounter with Jesus on the road to Damascus. Saul, who was on mission to persecute Christians in another city, repented and became Paul. In doing so, he became one of the biggest champions of the faith. The very next verse says something we discussed at length in chapter five,

> *But by the grace of God I am what I am, and His grace toward me was not in vain; but I labored more abundantly than they all, yet not I, but the grace of God which was with me.* — 1 Corinthians 15:10 (NKJV)

Repentance is a powerful force that can change the destinies of nations, and even of murderers like Paul. It is powerful enough to change the course of your life too.

All it takes is a decision on your part. You can decide today to repent from your old mindsets and move in an entirely new direction as you take the Kingdom of God by force.

Starting Small is OK

I want to leave you with this challenge. Get with God. If you know what He's been speaking to your heart to do, then repent. Push your excuses aside. Stop waiting for God to do it all for you. Commit to take some action to move in the direction that God is calling you.

It's OK if that first step of faith is really small.

Do you know what the first step of faith Lisa and I took when we realized that God was calling us to go to Scotland and start the Bible college campus there in Dumfries? I sent an email.

I just read it again as I was preparing my notes for this book. In that short email, I asked a Scottish pastor we had met when we traveled to that town if Lisa and I could have a short meeting with him and his wife.

I had no idea how he'd respond. And I remember being a little intimidated about clicking the send button because I didn't want to mess it up. But we've seen God do some amazing things since I hit send on that message all those years ago.

So, whatever it is that God is prompting you to respond to right now, take one step in that direction. That step is your faith in action. And as that step is effective, it will give you more confidence for the next step of faith. And the next one after that.

My email was the first small step of faith in a whole long chain of faith steps that spanned years, and led Lisa and I to Scotland, where we established a Bible college campus that continues transforming lives even today. Through us God raised up a powerhouse leadership team there in Scotland. Then God had us hand off that work to the team and move back here to America where He has more assignments for us.

I have no idea where your step of faith will ultimately lead you, but I promise you this: When you walk with God, it will be an amazing journey that you wouldn't change for anything in the world. And it sure beats where I was all those many years ago, sitting back waiting for God to do something and drop a miracle in my lap, while I lived a life no different from the unbelievers in the world around me.

Your time is now. Step up! Walk in boldness with God. Take the Kingdom of God by force!

My Prayer For You

As we close out this book, I would like to change things up a bit and pray for you. Hopefully that is OK.

> *Father, thank you so much for the hunger and determination for your Kingdom that you put in the heart of this reader. I ask that You unlock grace power in their lives. I know there is a great deal of work to be done in this season as You continue to expand Your Kingdom here on earth. Speak to this reader in a way that resonates with their heart. Show them the part of Your Kingdom You would have them take by force. Give them success in each faith step. Bless them even when they have missteps. Let your truth come alive in their soul so powerfully that it overflows onto all around them with so much blessing it cannot be contained.*

> *For I know the plans I have for you," declares the LORD, "plans to prosper you and not to harm you, plans to give you hope and a future.* — Jeremiah 29:11 (NIV)

About the Author

Chris Cree was a merchant marine officer and flew off of aircraft carriers in jets with the US Navy. After leaving the Navy he spent 12 years working on the docks in various marine cargo operations positions. In 2007 Chris turned his blogging hobby into a new career developing websites, both in his own business as a freelancer and as an employee of a rapidly growing firm. This job change provided the flexibility to eventually leave the coast where the ships were, move to the mountains and go to Bible college.

Chris and his wife Lisa founded NewCREEations Ministries in 2013 as a vehicle to answer God's call on their lives to guide believers into their full inheritance in the Kingdom of God. They lived in Scotland for a number of years as missionaries. While there, they established a local campus of an international Bible college. In 2021 God gave them a clear word to pass the baton to local leaders raised up on their team and return to the States.

Through NewCREEations, Chris and Lisa focus on ministering life-changing Bible teaching, helping believers experience the Kingdom of God and His goodness in practical ways which improve their lives. They travel and teach, publish books, and produce video content along with a variety of other materials. They are working on establishing and growing a new extension of NewCREEations Ministries called Kingdom Mindsets, a discipleship platform to fulfill the Great Commission by connecting anointed ministries with the Body of Christ.

You can learn more and contact them with questions or other inquiries via their NewCREEations.org website.

Also by Chris Cree

Rejecting Mammon: How to See Results From Your Giving

How to Believe Your Way to Supernatural Faith

Daily Reflections: 365 Powerful Devotions for Stronger Faith Every Day

Church Websites: How to Communicate the Gospel Effectively in a Social Media World

Short Read

Sovereignty of God: Is God Really in Control?

www.ingramcontent.com/pod-product-compliance
Lightning Source LLC
LaVergne TN
LVHW010502160826
845677LV00012B/2608